Preface or Foreword

In the vibrant and ever-evolving landscape of India's economy, the quest for financial freedom is a journey that many aspire to embark upon. It is a path filled with challenges and opportunities, requiring not just the acumen to navigate through the complexities of personal finance but also the wisdom to make informed decisions that pave the way to financial independence. "Master Your Finances: A Comprehensive Guide to Financial Freedom in India" is born out of this very essence—the desire to empower individuals with the knowledge and tools needed to take control of their financial destinies.

As the author of this guide, my journey into the realms of finance and business was not a matter of chance but a deliberate choice shaped by my academic pursuits and professional endeavors. Having embarked on an academic journey that spanned the disciplines of Business Administration and Law from GH Raisoni College, Nagpur, followed by a deep dive into Leadership in Organisation at the London School of Economics, I was equipped with a multifaceted understanding of business, finance, and the legal frameworks that govern them. Yet, it was the decade spent navigating the intricacies of doing business in India that truly honed my insights and perspectives on financial management.

This book is a distillation of the lessons learned, the challenges overcome, and the strategies that have stood the test of time. It is crafted with the Indian financial landscape in mind, acknowledging the unique challenges and opportunities that it presents. From understanding the basics of financial planning to navigating the complexities of investments, tax planning, and retirement, this guide aims to be your trusted companion on the journey to financial freedom.

Beyond the strategies and advice, this book is a testament to the belief that financial literacy is not just a skill but a fundamental right. It is the key to unlocking a future that is not only secure but also rich with the potential for growth and fulfillment. Whether you are taking your first steps into the world of finance or looking to refine your strategies for wealth management, this guide seeks to offer valuable insights that resonate with your aspirations.

It is with a sense of humility and purpose that I present "Master Your Finances" to you, the reader. May this book serve as a beacon, guiding you through the financial challenges and opportunities that lie ahead. Together, let us embark on this journey towards financial empowerment and freedom.

Warm regards,

Rahul Goyal

Acknowledgments

As I reflect on the journey that led to the creation of "Master Your Finances: A Comprehensive Guide to Financial Freedom in India," I am filled with gratitude for the numerous individuals who played pivotal roles in bringing this book to life. The process of writing this book has been a journey not just of intellectual exploration but also of profound personal growth. It is a journey that I did not undertake alone.

First and foremost, my heartfelt thanks go to my family, whose unwavering support and encouragement have been my constant source of strength and motivation. Their belief in my vision has been the bedrock upon which this endeavor was built. To my parents, for instilling in me the values of perseverance and diligence, and to my partner, for being my sounding board and my pillar of support, I owe a debt of gratitude that words cannot fully express.

I am profoundly grateful to my mentors and professors at GH Raisoni College, Nagpur, and the London School of Economics, whose invaluable guidance has shaped my understanding of business, law, and leadership. Their teachings have not only informed the insights shared in this book but have also inspired me to pursue excellence in all my endeavors.

A special word of thanks to my colleagues and friends in the business community, whose experiences and stories have enriched this book. Their openness in sharing their financial journeys has provided depth and relatability to the principles and strategies discussed herein.

I am also indebted to the team of professionals who worked tirelessly behind the scenes to bring this book to fruition. To my editor, whose keen eye and insightful suggestions have greatly enhanced the clarity and impact of this guide. To the designers and publishers, whose expertise has given this book its form and presence. Your dedication and professionalism have been instrumental in realizing this project.

Lastly, I extend my gratitude to you, the readers, for embarking on this journey with me. It is my sincere hope that this book empowers you to navigate the complexities of personal finance with confidence and clarity. Your engagement and feedback are not just invaluable to me—they are the very essence of this book's purpose.

To all who have contributed to this journey, whether directly or indirectly, I extend my deepest thanks. Your support, guidance, and encouragement have been the guiding lights on this path to financial empowerment.

With gratitude,

Rahul Goyal

Dedication

To my father,

and all the torchbearers in my life,

who illuminated the path with wisdom and love,

guiding me through darkness and light.

This book is dedicated to you.

Here's a chapter-wise index for "Master Your Finances: A Comprehensive Guide to Financial Freedom in India":

Introduction
- Welcome to Financial Freedom
- The Purpose and Structure of This Book

Chapter 1: Understanding Financial Basics
- Why Financial Literacy Matters
- Setting Financial Goals
- The Art of Budgeting
- The Significance of an Emergency Fund
- Making Informed Financial Decisions
- Laying the Groundwork for Financial Success

Chapter 2: Managing Debt Wisely
- The Double-Edged Sword of Debt
- Prioritizing Your Debt Repayments
- Navigating Through Debt Traps
- The Art of Negotiating with Creditors
- Building and Maintaining a Healthy Credit Score
- Creating a Sustainable Debt Management Plan
- Transforming Debt from Burden to Opportunity

Chapter 3: Building Wealth through Investments
- The Essence of Investing in India
- Navigating the Stock Market
- The Power of Mutual Funds
- Real Estate as a Tangible Asset
- Exploring Alternative Investments
- Investment Strategies and Risk Management
- Maximizing Returns: Tips and Tricks

Chapter 4: Tax Planning Strategies
- Understanding the Indian Tax Landscape

- Maximizing Deductions and Exemptions
- Optimizing Investment Choices for Tax Efficiency
- Long-term Tax Planning for Retirement
- Tax Planning for High Net-worth Individuals (HNIs)
- Leveraging Technology in Tax Planning

Chapter 5: Retirement Planning and Pension
- Envisioning Your Retirement
- Retirement Savings Vehicles in India
- The Power of Compounding in Retirement Savings
- Investment Strategies for Retirement
- Managing Risks in Retirement Planning
- Estate Planning: Securing Your Legacy

Chapter 6: Achieving Financial Freedom
- The Essence of Financial Freedom
- Setting the Foundation: Control Over Finances
- Creating Passive Income Streams
- Investing Wisely: Building Your Wealth
- Lifestyle Design: Living a Life of Abundance
- Adopting a Proactive Mindset

Chapter 7: Navigating Economic Challenges
- Understanding Economic Challenges
- Building a Financial Safety Net
- Strategies for Weathering Job Loss
- Combating Inflation
- Navigating Market Downturns
- Seizing Opportunities in Challenging Times
- Cultivating Financial Resilience

Chapter 8: Cultivating Healthy Financial Habits
- The Bedrock of Financial Success: Positive Money Habits

- Mindful Spending: The Art of Financial Consciousness
- The Power of Budgeting: Navigating Your Financial Roadmap
- Automating Your Finances: The Path to Effortless Management
- Investing in Financial Education: The Key to Empowerment
- Fostering a Community of Financial Wellness

Glossary
- Key Financial Terms Explained

FAQs Section
- Answers to Common Financial Questions

Recommended Reading and Resources
- Further Learning and Exploration

About the Author
- Background and Insights

Testimonials and Reviews
- Reader and Professional Feedback

This structured index provides a clear roadmap through the book, ensuring readers can easily navigate the comprehensive guide to achieving financial freedom in India.

Title: "Master Your Finances: A Comprehensive Guide to Financial Freedom in India"

Introduction

Welcome to "Master Your Finances," your go-to guide for navigating the complex world of personal finance and achieving financial freedom in India. In this book, we will explore essential principles, actionable strategies, and expert insights to help you take control of your finances, build wealth, and secure your future.

Chapter 1: Understanding Financial Basics

In this chapter, we'll lay the foundation for your financial journey by covering the fundamentals of personal finance. We'll discuss the importance of setting financial goals, creating a budget, and establishing emergency funds. By understanding these basics, you'll be better equipped to make informed financial decisions and lay the groundwork for financial success.

Let's embark on the journey to financial freedom and literacy by diving deep into the essentials of personal finance. In this inaugural chapter, we lay the foundation stone of your financial edifice. As we navigate through the complexities of personal finance, we aim not only to educate but also to empower you. By understanding the importance of setting financial goals, creating a budget, and establishing emergency funds, you'll be armed with the knowledge to make informed decisions that will pave the path to financial success.

Understanding Financial Basics

Why Financial Literacy Matters

In today's fast-paced world, financial literacy stands as a beacon of empowerment. It's the knowledge that enables us to make informed and effective decisions with all of our financial resources. For many, financial independence is a goal, but to achieve it, one must first traverse the path of financial literacy. Understanding the basics of personal finance is not just about managing money; it's about securing a future that is free from financial stress.

Setting Financial Goals

The journey to financial wisdom begins with setting clear, achievable goals. These are the lighthouses guiding you through the stormy seas of financial decisions. Goals can range from short-term objectives, such as saving for a vacation or paying off credit card debt, to long-term aspirations like buying a home, funding education, or ensuring a comfortable retirement. The key is specificity and realism; goals should be SMART - Specific, Measurable, Achievable, Relevant, and Time-bound.

The Art of Budgeting

Budgeting is the cornerstone of personal financial planning. It is an art that balances income against expenses, ensuring that we live within our means while saving for the future. A well-crafted budget provides a clear picture of where your money is going, highlighting opportunities to cut back and save. It's not about restriction, but about making informed choices and prioritizing what's truly important to you.

The Significance of an Emergency Fund

Life is unpredictable. An emergency fund acts as a financial safety net designed to cover unexpected expenses, such as medical emergencies, job loss, or urgent home repairs. Ideally, it should cover three to six months' worth of living expenses. Establishing and maintaining an emergency fund is a fundamental step in protecting yourself and your loved ones from unforeseen financial shocks.

Making Informed Financial Decisions

Armed with the knowledge of financial basics, you're now in a position to make informed decisions that align with your goals and budget. Whether it's choosing the right insurance policies, investing in the stock market, or simply deciding between buying or leasing a car, each decision you make will impact your financial future.

Laying the Groundwork for Financial Success

Understanding these financial basics is akin to laying a strong foundation for a building. It's the groundwork upon which your financial house will stand tall and unshaken by the tempests of life. This chapter serves as your starting point in the fascinating journey of personal finance. As we progress, we will delve deeper into each aspect, unraveling the complexities and equipping you with the tools you need to achieve financial success.

By embracing these fundamentals, you're not just planning for your future; you're taking the first step towards financial empowerment and independence. As we continue this journey together, remember that financial literacy is not a destination but a continuous path of growth and learning.

Chapter 2: Managing Debt Wisely

Debt can be a significant obstacle on the path to financial freedom. In this chapter, we'll explore strategies for managing debt effectively, including prioritizing repayments, avoiding common debt traps, and building a healthy credit score. By taking control of your debt, you'll pave the way for a brighter financial future.

In the pursuit of financial freedom, managing debt is akin to navigating through treacherous waters. It requires precision, discipline, and a well-thought-out strategy. This chapter delves into the complexities of debt, offering you the tools and knowledge to wield it wisely, rather than allowing it to become a hindrance on your journey to financial prosperity. We'll explore the principles of prioritizing repayments, steering clear of common debt traps, and cultivating a robust credit score, setting the stage for a brighter, more secure financial future.

Chapter 2: Managing Debt Wisely

The Double-Edged Sword of Debt

Debt is a powerful tool in your financial arsenal but wielding it carelessly can inflict damage on your financial health. Understanding the nature of different debts—recognizing the distinction between 'good debt', which can be an investment in your future, such as a mortgage or education loan, and 'bad debt', like high-interest credit card debt, is crucial. This understanding forms the basis of effective debt management.

Prioritizing Your Debt Repayments

Not all debts are created equal. Some carry exorbitant interest rates that can quickly become overwhelming, while others offer more manageable terms. The 'avalanche' method, which focuses on paying off debts with the highest interest rates first, and the 'snowball' method, which involves settling smaller debts first for psychological wins, are two proven strategies for debt repayment. Choosing the right strategy depends on your financial situation and psychological preference.

Navigating Through Debt Traps

In the modern consumer economy, it's easy to fall into debt traps. From enticing credit card offers to the allure of 'buy now, pay later' schemes, these traps can derail your financial plans. Recognizing and avoiding these pitfalls requires vigilance and a strong understanding of the terms and conditions of any financial product. Remember, if an offer seems too good to be true, it likely is.

The Art of Negotiating with Creditors

If you find yourself struggling with debt, remember that negotiation is always an option. Many creditors prefer to settle for a payment plan that works for both parties rather than pursue legal action or write off the debt as a loss. Approach negotiations with honesty, armed with a realistic proposal for repayment. This can not only alleviate your current financial burden but also help preserve your credit score.

Building and Maintaining a Healthy Credit Score

Your credit score is a reflection of your financial reliability and a key factor in securing future loans on favorable terms. Paying bills on time, keeping credit card balances low, and avoiding unnecessary new credit lines are essential practices for maintaining a healthy credit score. Moreover, regularly monitoring your credit report can help you catch and rectify any inaccuracies that may be affecting your score negatively.

Creating a Sustainable Debt Management Plan

A sustainable debt management plan is the cornerstone of financial stability. It involves budgeting wisely, setting aside emergency funds to avoid new debts, and consistently reviewing and adjusting your plan as your financial situation evolves. Remember, managing debt is not just about making repayments; it's about changing the behaviors that led to debt in the first place.

Transforming Debt from Burden to Opportunity

Effectively managed debt can be a stepping stone rather than a stumbling block. By employing the strategies outlined in this chapter, you can transform debt from a source of stress into an opportunity for growth. The journey towards financial freedom is not about avoiding debt altogether but about mastering its management.

By taking control of your debt, you're not just clearing a path to financial freedom; you're also building the resilience and discipline that characterize wise financial stewardship. As we continue to explore the pillars of personal finance in the chapters that follow, remember that managing debt wisely is not a destination but a continuous journey towards a brighter financial future.

Chapter 3: Building Wealth through Investments

Investing is a key component of wealth-building. In this chapter, we'll delve into various investment options available in India, including stocks, mutual funds, real estate, and alternative investments. We'll discuss investment strategies, risk management techniques, and tips for maximizing returns. By harnessing the power of investments, you can grow your wealth and achieve your financial goals.

Embarking on the journey of building wealth is an exhilarating adventure, and investing serves as the vehicle that propels you towards your financial aspirations. In the vast and dynamic landscape of India, a myriad of investment options beckons, each with its unique allure and potential pitfalls. This chapter is your compass, guiding you through the terrain of stocks, mutual funds, real estate, and the intriguing world of alternative investments. We will navigate through investment strategies, risk management, and the art of maximizing returns. By the chapter's end, you'll be equipped with the insights needed to harness the power of investments, setting the stage for wealth accumulation and the realization of your financial dreams.

Chapter 3: Building Wealth through Investments

The Essence of Investing in India

India's economic landscape is a fertile ground for investors, offering a diverse array of opportunities from the bustling stock markets in Mumbai to the tangible asset class of real estate and beyond. The key to unlocking these opportunities lies in understanding the nuances of each investment option and aligning them with your financial goals and risk tolerance.

Navigating the Stock Market

The Indian stock market, with its two major exchanges, the Bombay Stock Exchange (BSE) and the National Stock Exchange (NSE), offers a platform for wealth creation through equity investments. While investing in stocks can provide substantial returns, it requires a deep understanding of market trends, company performance, and economic indicators. Embracing a disciplined approach to investing, coupled with thorough research, can help mitigate risks and enhance the potential for gains.

The Power of Mutual Funds

Mutual funds in India have emerged as a favored investment vehicle for those seeking diversification and professional management of their funds. By pooling resources with other investors, individuals can gain access to a broader range of securities than would be feasible to manage on their own. Understanding the types of mutual funds available, from equity and debt funds to hybrid and index funds, is crucial in selecting the right fund that matches your investment horizon and risk appetite.

Real Estate as a Tangible Asset

Investing in real estate offers the dual advantage of capital appreciation and potential rental income, making it an attractive option for long-term wealth building. The Indian real estate market, with its diverse options ranging from residential and commercial properties to land, requires due diligence and a grasp of market dynamics. Factors such as location, demand-supply equilibrium, and future development plans play a significant role in influencing the profitability of real estate investments.

Exploring Alternative Investments

Alternative investments encompass a wide range of options outside the traditional realms of stocks, bonds, and real estate. This includes commodities, private equity, hedge funds, and even art and collectibles. While these investments can offer higher returns and diversification benefits, they also come with higher risks and often require a more substantial initial investment. Venturing into the world of alternative investments necessitates a sophisticated understanding of these markets and a willingness to explore uncharted territories.

Investment Strategies and Risk Management

Crafting a successful investment strategy involves more than just selecting the right assets. It's about aligning these choices with your financial objectives, investment horizon, and risk tolerance. Diversification stands as a pillar of effective risk management, ensuring that your investment portfolio can withstand market volatility and economic downturns. Regularly reviewing and rebalancing your portfolio is also essential to maintaining its alignment with your financial goals.

Maximizing Returns: Tips and Tricks

Maximizing your investment returns is not solely about chasing high-risk options. It's about smart decision-making, which includes taking advantage of tax-saving investments, leveraging the power of compounding by investing early, and staying informed about market trends and financial news. Patience and persistence are virtues in the investment world, often rewarded with substantial long-term gains.

Conclusion: Your Path to Wealth Building

Investing is more than a mere transaction; it's a journey towards financial empowerment. As you embark on this journey in India, equipped with the knowledge and strategies outlined in this chapter, remember that building wealth is a marathon, not a sprint. By making informed investment choices, managing risks wisely, and staying committed to your financial goals, you're setting the stage for a future rich in financial success and personal fulfillment.

Chapter 4: Tax Planning Strategies

Taxes play a significant role in your financial life. In this chapter, we'll explore tax planning strategies tailored to the Indian context, including maximizing deductions, optimizing investment choices, and long-term tax planning for retirement. By understanding the tax landscape and leveraging available incentives, you can minimize your tax burden and keep more money in your pocket.

Navigating the labyrinth of taxation can often seem daunting, but mastering this aspect of your finances can lead to substantial savings and significantly bolster your wealth-building efforts. In the vibrant economic landscape of India, where tax laws are intricate and ever-evolving, being adept at tax planning is not just beneficial—it's essential. This chapter demystifies tax planning, offering a comprehensive guide tailored to the Indian context. We delve into maximizing deductions, optimizing investment choices, and crafting a long-term tax strategy that harmonizes with your retirement plans. By the end of this chapter, you'll possess the knowledge to navigate the tax landscape confidently, leveraging every available incentive to minimize your tax liability and enhance your financial well-being.

Chapter 4: Tax Planning Strategies

Understanding the Indian Tax Landscape

The Indian tax system is a complex web of direct and indirect taxes, with the Income Tax Act of 1961 at its core.

Understanding the basics, including the different income tax slabs and the distinction between exempt, deductible, and taxable income, is the first step in effective tax planning. This foundational knowledge enables you to navigate the complexities of the tax system and identify opportunities to reduce your tax liability.

Maximizing Deductions and Exemptions

India's tax laws offer a myriad of deductions and exemptions designed to encourage savings, investment, and economic growth. Familiarizing yourself with these provisions can lead to significant tax savings. Key sections of the Income Tax Act, such as 80C, 80D, and 80E, allow deductions for specific investments, insurance premiums, and education loans, respectively. Harnessing these provisions to their fullest potential requires strategic planning and an understanding of their respective limits and conditions.

Optimizing Investment Choices for Tax Efficiency

Certain investment vehicles in India offer not just attractive returns but also tax advantages. Equity Linked Savings Schemes (ELSS), Public Provident Fund (PPF), National Pension System (NPS), and Sukanya Samriddhi Yojana are examples of investments that not only grow your wealth but also reduce your tax burden. Selecting the right mix of these investments can optimize your tax savings while aligning with your financial goals and risk tolerance.

Long-term Tax Planning for Retirement

Planning for retirement should include a strategy for minimizing taxes on your retirement income. The NPS is a critical component of this strategy, offering tax benefits on contributions, accumulated wealth, and even partial withdrawals. Moreover, choosing the right annuity plan upon retirement can also impact your tax liability. Long-term tax planning involves a comprehensive approach, considering the tax implications of your retirement savings and investments well before you reach retirement age.

Tax Planning for High Net-worth Individuals (HNIs)

For high net-worth individuals, tax planning takes on additional complexity. Strategies such as forming family trusts, investing in insurance products like ULIPs, and exploring opportunities for tax-efficient wealth transfer can play a pivotal role in minimizing tax liability. Professional advice from tax consultants and financial advisors becomes indispensable in navigating the high-stakes world of HNI tax planning.

Leveraging Technology in Tax Planning

In today's digital age, numerous tools and platforms can simplify tax planning. From online tax calculators to investment tracking software, technology offers a way to manage your taxes more efficiently. Moreover, the Indian government's push towards digitization in tax filings and transactions provides additional transparency and ease in managing tax obligations.

Conclusion: Elevating Your Financial Acumen through Tax Planning

Tax planning is an integral part of financial planning, offering a pathway to reduce your tax liability and enhance your savings. In the context of India's intricate tax system, being proactive, informed, and strategic about your tax planning can lead to substantial financial benefits. By applying the strategies discussed in this chapter, you're not just saving on taxes; you're taking a significant step towards financial literacy and empowerment, setting the stage for a future of financial success and stability.

Chapter 5: Retirement Planning and Pension

Planning for retirement is essential to ensure financial security in your golden years. In this chapter, we'll discuss retirement goals, retirement savings vehicles, and investment strategies for building a nest egg. Whether you're just starting your career or nearing retirement age, it's never too early or too late to plan for retirement.

As you journey through life's myriad phases, planning for retirement emerges as a pivotal aspect of financial stewardship, ensuring tranquility and security in your golden years. This chapter unfurls the roadmap to a serene retirement, tailored for every stage of your professional life. From delineating retirement goals to selecting the right savings vehicles and crafting investment strategies, we cover the gamut of planning essentials. Whether you're embarking on your career or standing on the cusp of retirement, the axiom holds true—it's never too premature or too late to architect your retirement dreams.

Chapter 5: Retirement Planning and Pension

Envisioning Your Retirement

The first step in retirement planning is to envision your retirement lifestyle. Do you see yourself traveling the world, pursuing hobbies, or perhaps engaging in philanthropy? Estimating the financial resources required to support your retirement lifestyle is crucial. This involves calculating potential expenses, considering inflation, and planning for healthcare needs. Crafting a vivid, detailed vision of your retirement not only motivates but also helps in setting precise financial targets.

Retirement Savings Vehicles in India

India offers a plethora of retirement savings options, each with its unique features and tax benefits. The Employees' Provident Fund (EPF) and the Public Provident Fund (PPF) are foundational pillars for retirement savings, offering secure, tax-efficient growth. The National Pension System (NPS) stands out for its flexibility and potential for higher returns, catering to those willing to navigate the equity market's waves. Understanding the nuances of these vehicles and how they fit into your retirement plan is paramount.

The Power of Compounding in Retirement Savings

The essence of building a substantial retirement nest egg lies in harnessing the power of compounding. Starting early amplifies this effect, transforming modest savings into significant sums over time. Even if you embark on this journey later in life, strategic investments and maximizing contributions to your retirement accounts can still yield impressive results. Compounding is the silent guardian that nurtures your retirement dreams into reality.

Investment Strategies for Retirement

Diversification is the cornerstone of any robust investment strategy, especially for retirement planning. A balanced mix of equity, debt, and other asset classes can optimize returns while mitigating risks. As you approach retirement, shifting towards more conservative investments can help preserve capital. Regularly reviewing and adjusting your investment portfolio in line with your retirement timeline and financial goals ensures that your strategy evolves with your needs.

Managing Risks in Retirement Planning

Retirement planning is not without its risks, from market volatility to inflation eroding purchasing power. Incorporating risk management strategies, such as maintaining an emergency fund, opting for insurance coverages, and planning for longevity, can safeguard your retirement savings. Being informed and prepared for these risks allows you to navigate them with confidence.

Estate Planning: Securing Your Legacy

An often overlooked but essential aspect of retirement planning is estate planning. It ensures that your assets are distributed according to your wishes and provides for your loved ones after your demise. Drafting a will, setting up trusts, and making clear nominations for your investments are critical steps in securing your financial legacy.

Conclusion: The Journey to a Fulfilling Retirement

Retirement planning is a dynamic, ongoing process that adjusts to life's changes and financial landscapes. It's a journey of foresight, discipline, and strategic planning, requiring attention and care at every stage of your career. By engaging in thorough planning, informed investing, and diligent saving, you're not just preparing for a future of financial security—you're paving the way for a retirement filled with peace, purpose, and prosperity.

Your retirement years are a testament to a life well-lived and a career well-spent. Through meticulous planning and smart financial decisions, you can ensure that this chapter of your life is marked by fulfillment and joy, free from financial worries.

Chapter 6: Achieving Financial Freedom

Financial freedom is the ultimate goal of our financial journey. In this chapter, we'll explore what it means to achieve financial independence and early retirement. We'll discuss steps to take control of your finances, create passive income streams, and design a life of abundance and fulfillment. By adopting a proactive mindset and implementing proven strategies, you can chart your course to financial freedom.

---Achieving financial freedom is akin to conquering the highest summit of personal finance. It represents not just the culmination of wise financial decisions and disciplined saving but also the beginning of a life defined by choice, abundance, and fulfillment. In this pivotal chapter, we embark on a quest to unravel the essence of financial independence and early retirement. We'll navigate through the strategies to master your finances, cultivate passive income streams, and craft a life rich in possibilities. This journey calls for a proactive mindset, armed with knowledge and determination, to steer your financial destiny towards the shore of freedom.

Chapter 6: Achieving Financial Freedom

The Essence of Financial Freedom

Financial freedom is the state where your wealth sufficiently covers your living expenses, liberating you from the need to work for money. It's about achieving a level of financial security that allows you to pursue your passions, interests, and dreams without monetary constraints. This liberty isn't just about having wealth but about understanding and leveraging it to create a life that aligns with your deepest values and aspirations.

***Setting the Foundation: Control Over Finances*5**

The bedrock of financial freedom is establishing control over your finances. This involves meticulous budgeting, eliminating debt, and cultivating a savings mindset. It's about making intentional decisions with your money, ensuring every rupee serves a purpose towards your ultimate goal. Understanding the flow of your finances, from income to expenses, investments to savings, is critical in this quest.

***Creating Passive Income Streams*5**

Passive income—money earned with minimal ongoing effort—is the cornerstone of financial independence. Diversifying your income sources ensures a steady flow of money, reducing reliance on a traditional job. Investments in dividend-paying stocks, rental properties, royalties from intellectual property, or online businesses can serve as vehicles driving you towards financial freedom. The goal is to build these streams to a point where they fully cover your living expenses.

sInvesting Wisely: Building Your Wealthx

The path to financial freedom is paved with smart investments. It's about leveraging the power of compounding, understanding market dynamics, and making informed choices that align with your risk tolerance and time horizon. Whether it's equity, real estate, mutual funds, or alternative investments, each decision must be made with an eye towards long-term wealth creation and capital preservation.

Lifestyle Design: Living a Life of Abundance

Financial freedom offers the canvas to design a life of abundance, but it requires a conscious effort to live below your means and prioritize what truly brings happiness. It's a delicate balance between frugality and fulfillment, ensuring that your spending aligns with your values and goals. This lifestyle design isn't about deprivation but about making thoughtful choices that enhance your life's quality without jeopardizing financial independence.

Adopting a Proactive Mindset

A proactive mindset is the fuel that drives your journey to financial freedom. It's about taking responsibility for your financial destiny, continuously seeking knowledge, and being prepared to adapt to changing circumstances. This mindset encourages constant growth, learning, and the resilience to face financial challenges head-on.

Conclusion: Charting Your Course to Financial Freedom

Achieving financial freedom is a journey marked by deliberate choices, disciplined saving, and strategic investing. It's a testament to the power of a proactive mindset and the relentless pursuit of your financial goals. As you forge ahead, remember that financial freedom is not merely a destination but a way of living—a life rich in choices, free from financial constraints, and full of potential for growth and happiness.

This chapter is not just a guide but a call to action—to embrace the principles of financial independence and to craft a life of purpose and abundance. Your journey to financial freedom is both unique and universal, a path walked by many but defined by the individual steps you choose to take.

Chapter 7: Navigating Economic Challenges

Economic challenges are inevitable, but they don't have to derail your financial plans. In this chapter, we'll discuss strategies for weathering economic storms, including job loss, inflation, and market downturns. By building resilience and seizing opportunities in challenging times, you can emerge stronger and more financially secure.

---In the voyage of personal finance, encountering economic tempests is inevitable. Yet, it's your preparation and response to these challenges that determine your financial vessel's resilience and course. This chapter is dedicated to charting a path through economic challenges, equipping you with strategies to not just endure but thrive amid adversity. From navigating job loss and battling inflation to steering through market downturns, we lay down the principles of financial resilience and opportunity. By adopting a proactive and strategic approach, you can transform potential crises into catalysts for growth, emerging on the other side more financially secure and empowered.

Chapter 7: Navigating Economic Challenges

Understanding Economic Challenges

Economic challenges often arrive unannounced, manifesting as job losses, rampant inflation, or severe market downturns. These events can erode purchasing power, diminish savings, and unsettle financial markets. However, understanding these challenges not as setbacks but as integral parts of the economic cycle can shift your perspective, enabling you to prepare and respond effectively.

Building a Financial Safety Net

The cornerstone of navigating economic challenges is a robust financial safety net. This entails establishing an emergency fund covering at least six months of living expenses, ensuring you have a financial cushion to rely on during unforeseen crises. Additionally, diversifying your income streams can bolster your financial resilience, reducing the impact of job loss or market fluctuations.

Strategies for Weathering Job Loss

The specter of job loss looms large in economic downturns, making career resilience crucial. This involves continuously upgrading your skills, networking, and maintaining a professional online presence. Should job loss occur, it's important to manage your finances tightly, prioritizing essential expenses and tapping into your emergency fund judiciously.

Combating Inflation

Inflation can stealthily erode your purchasing power, making strategic adjustments necessary. Investing in assets that historically outpace inflation, such as equities or real estate, can safeguard your wealth. Additionally, revisiting and adjusting your budget to prioritize essential spending and cut non-essential expenses can help manage the impact of inflation on your daily finances.

Navigating Market Downturns

Market downturns, while challenging, are not uncommon. Viewing these as temporary setbacks rather than permanent losses can be beneficial. Staying the course with a diversified investment portfolio, avoiding panic selling, and seizing opportunities to buy quality assets at lower prices can enhance your financial position in the long run.

Seizing Opportunities in Challenging Times

Economic challenges, while daunting, can present unique opportunities. Market downturns can offer chances to invest in undervalued assets, while economic recoveries can accelerate growth in certain sectors. Maintaining a balanced and informed perspective allows you to identify and capitalize on these opportunities, turning potential threats into avenues for growth.

Cultivating Financial Resilience

At the heart of navigating economic challenges is financial resilience—the ability to withstand and adapt to financial adversities. This resilience is cultivated through informed decision-making, continuous learning, and an unwavering commitment to your financial goals. It involves not just surviving economic challenges but using them as stepping stones to financial empowerment and security.

Conclusion: Emerging Stronger from Economic Challenges

Economic challenges test your financial resilience and adaptability but also offer opportunities for growth and learning. By building a financial safety net, diversifying your income, and adopting a proactive approach to investment and budgeting, you can navigate these challenges effectively. Remember, economic storms are temporary; with preparation and perspective, you can emerge stronger, wiser, and on a firmer financial footing.

As we conclude this chapter, let it be a beacon guiding you through economic turbulence, reminding you that with the right strategies and mindset, you can not only survive but thrive in the face of adversity.

Chapter 8: Cultivating Healthy Financial Habits

Lasting financial success requires cultivating healthy habits and mindset. In this final chapter, we'll explore practical tips for developing positive money habits, practicing mindful spending, and automating your finances. By adopting a proactive approach to your financial life, you can set yourself up for long-term success and abundance.

**The odyssey towards financial prosperity is not solely charted through strategic investments or meticulous planning; it's deeply rooted in the everyday habits that sculpt our financial landscape. This concluding chapter serves as a cornerstone, laying out the blueprint for cultivating healthy financial habits that foster a mindset of abundance and success. Herein, we explore practical strategies for nurturing positive money habits, embracing mindful spending, and streamlining your financial management through automation. This guide is not merely about financial acumen—it's a transformative approach to embedding financial health into the fabric of your life, setting the stage for a future replete with prosperity and financial freedom.

Chapter 8: Cultivating Healthy Financial Habits

The Bedrock of Financial Success: Positive Money Habits

Financial success is an edifice built on the foundation of daily habits. It begins with setting clear, achievable goals and breaking them down into actionable steps. Regularly reviewing your financial progress, celebrating milestones, and adjusting your plan as necessary keeps you aligned with your long-term objectives. Establishing a routine for financial check-ins—be it weekly, monthly, or quarterly—ensures you remain on track and can make timely adjustments.

Mindful Spending: The Art of Financial Consciousness

At the heart of financial well-being lies mindful spending—a practice of conscious consumption that aligns your financial decisions with your values and goals. It involves questioning the necessity and value of every purchase, distinguishing between wants and needs, and understanding the long-term impact of your spending choices. Mindful spending isn't about austerity; it's about making informed decisions that enhance your life's quality without compromising your financial health.

The Power of Budgeting: Navigating Your Financial Roadmap

Budgeting is the compass that guides your financial journey, offering clarity and control over your money. A well-structured budget provides a snapshot of your financial health, enabling you to prioritize expenses, allocate savings, and identify areas for improvement. Embracing budgeting as a regular practice demystifies your finances, empowering you with the knowledge to make informed decisions and adjust course as needed.

Automating Your Finances: The Path to Effortless Management

In the age of digital finance, automating your financial management can significantly enhance efficiency and reduce the likelihood of errors or oversights. From automating bill payments to setting up automatic transfers to savings and investment accounts, technology can streamline your financial operations, ensuring you never miss a payment or opportunity to save. Automation not only simplifies financial management but also fortifies your commitment to saving and investing, making it an effortless part of your routine.

Investing in Financial Education: The Key to Empowerment

Knowledge is the currency of empowerment in the realm of personal finance. Investing time in financial education—through books, courses, workshops, or online resources—equips you with the tools to make informed decisions, stay abreast of economic trends, and navigate the complexities of the financial world with confidence. Continuous learning fosters a growth mindset, enabling you to adapt to changing financial landscapes and seize opportunities for growth.

Fostering a Community of Financial Wellness

Surrounding yourself with a community that values financial wellness can amplify your success. Engaging with like-minded individuals offers a platform for sharing knowledge, experiences, and support. Whether it's through online forums, local clubs, or financial literacy programs, being part of a community fosters accountability, inspiration, and a sense of belonging on your financial journey.

Conclusion: The Journey to Financial Flourishment

As we conclude this guide, remember that cultivating healthy financial habits is a journey of continuous growth, reflection, and adaptation. By embracing mindful spending, automating your finances, and committing to lifelong learning, you set the foundation for lasting financial success. Let these principles guide you towards a future where financial freedom and abundance are not just aspirations but realities of your everyday life.

Your financial story is one of empowerment, resilience, and triumph. As you turn the page to the next chapter of your life, carry forward the lessons and habits that will illuminate your path to financial prosperity and fulfillment.

Glossary

This glossary is designed to help you familiarize yourself with key financial terms used throughout "Master Your Finances: A Comprehensive Guide to Financial Freedom in India." Understanding these terms is essential for navigating the complexities of personal finance and achieving financial literacy.

- **Asset:** Anything of value owned by an individual or corporation that can be used for future benefit or generating income.
- **Budget**: A plan that outlines an individual's or organization's financial objectives and the strategies for achieving them, including income, expenses, savings, and investments.
- **Compound Interest**: The process in which the interest earned on an amount of money is reinvested, so that in subsequent periods, interest is earned on the interest from previous periods as well as the principal amount.
- **Credit Score**: A numerical expression based on a level analysis of a person's credit files, representing the creditworthiness of an individual. A higher score implies better credit decisions and it can make creditors more confident that you will repay your future debts as agreed.
- **Debt:** Money owed by one party to another under the condition that it will be paid back at a later date, typically with interest.
- **Diversification:** An investment strategy that spreads investments across various financial instruments,

industries, and other categories to reduce exposure to any single asset or risk.
- **Emergency Fund**: A reserve of money set aside to cover the financial surprises life throws your way, such as losing your job or facing unexpected medical expenses.
- **Equity:** Ownership interest in a company, typically in the form of stocks, representing a claim on the company's assets and earnings.
- **Inflation**: The rate at which the general level of prices for goods and services is rising, and, subsequently, purchasing power is falling.
- **Investment:** The action or process of investing money for profit or material result.
- **Liquidity**: The ease with which an asset, or security, can be converted into ready cash without affecting its market price.
- **Mutual Fund:** An investment vehicle made up of a pool of funds collected from many investors for the purpose of investing in securities such as stocks, bonds, money market instruments, and other assets.
- **Net Worth**: The total assets minus total outside liabilities of an individual or a company, used as a measure of financial health.
- **Portfolio**: A range of investments held by a person or organization.
- **Risk Tolerance:** An individual investor's capacity to endure loss of some or all invested capital.
- **Savings:** The portion of disposable income not spent on consumption of goods and services, set aside for future use.
- **Stock:** A type of security that signifies ownership in a corporation and represents a claim on part of the corporation's assets and earnings.

- **Tax Deduction**: A reduction of income that is able to be taxed, typically as the result of expenses, particularly those incurred to produce additional income.

Remember, mastering the language of finance is the first step towards becoming financially literate and achieving financial freedom. This glossary serves as a foundation for understanding the principles discussed in this book and applying them to your financial journey.

FAQs Section

In this section, we've compiled a list of frequently asked questions to help clarify common queries you might have as you navigate through "Master Your Finances: A Comprehensive Guide to Financial Freedom in India." These questions cover a broad range of topics addressed in the book, offering succinct insights to enhance your understanding and application of financial principles.

1. What is Financial Freedom?

Financial freedom is the state of having sufficient personal wealth to live, without having to work actively for basic necessities. For financially independent people, their assets generate income that is greater than their expenses.

2. How Can I Start Investing with a Limited Budget?

Starting small is better than not starting at all. Consider beginning with mutual funds, particularly systematic investment plans (SIPs), which allow you to invest a small, fixed amount regularly. It's also wise to explore digital platforms that offer micro-investment opportunities in stocks and mutual funds.

3. What's the Best Way to Create a Budget?

The best budget is one that you can stick to. Start by tracking your income and expenses to understand where your money goes. Then, categorize your expenses into necessities, wants, and savings/investments. Use the 50/30/20 rule as a guideline: 50% on needs, 30% on wants, and at least 20% on savings and debt repayment.

4. How Much Should I Save in My Emergency Fund?

It's generally recommended to save three to six months' worth of living expenses in an emergency fund. This can vary based on your job stability, the number of income earners in your household, and your overall financial obligations.

5. How Do I Improve My Credit Score?

Improving your credit score involves several steps: paying your bills on time, reducing the amount of debt you owe, keeping old credit cards open to maintain a long credit history, and limiting new credit applications. Regularly checking your credit report for errors and addressing them promptly is also key.

6. What Are Some Common Debt Repayment Strategies?

The "snowball" method (paying off debts from smallest to largest to gain momentum) and the "avalanche" method (focusing on debts with the highest interest rates first) are two effective strategies. Choosing between them depends on what motivates you most: quick wins or saving on interest.

7. Is Real Estate a Good Investment Option?

Real estate can be a good investment if you do your homework. It provides potential for rental income and capital appreciation. However, it requires significant capital upfront and can be less liquid than other investment forms. It's important to consider your long-term goals and market conditions before investing in real estate.

8. How Can I Plan for Retirement?

Start by envisioning your desired retirement lifestyle and estimate the funds you'll need. Take advantage of retirement savings plans like the Employees' Provident Fund (EPF) and National Pension System (NPS). Investing in a diversified portfolio and periodically reviewing your retirement plan can also help ensure that you are on track to meet your goals.

9. What Should I Know About Taxes and Investments?

Understanding how your investments are taxed is crucial. Some investments offer tax benefits, which can enhance your returns. Familiarize yourself with terms like short-term and long-term capital gains, and consider seeking advice from a tax professional to make tax-efficient investment choices.

10. How Can I Cultivate Healthy Financial Habits?
Cultivating healthy financial habits involves setting clear goals, creating and sticking to a budget, saving regularly, investing wisely, and continuously educating yourself about personal finance. It's also important to regularly review your financial plan to adjust for any life changes or shifts in financial goals.

This FAQs section aims to address common questions and concerns, providing you with quick insights to better manage your finances. For more detailed explanations and guidance, refer to the respective chapters in this book.

Recommended Reading and Resources

Embarking on the journey towards financial freedom is both exhilarating and demanding. To aid in your quest, "Master Your Finances: A Comprehensive Guide to Financial Freedom in India" has curated a list of recommended readings and resources. These materials have been selected to deepen your understanding of personal finance, investment, tax planning, and more. They complement the principles and strategies discussed in this book, offering a broader perspective on achieving financial independence.

Books

"Rich Dad Poor Dad" by Robert T. Kiyosaki - A classic personal finance book that contrasts the financial philosophies of the author's two "fathers." It discusses the importance of financial education, investing, and building wealth.

"The Intelligent Investor" by Benjamin Graham - Widely regarded as the bible of value investing, this book offers insights into the philosophy of "value investing" –

investing in undervalued stocks that show true potential for long-term growth.

"Thinking, Fast and Slow" by Daniel Kahneman - This book delves into the various ways our minds make decisions, including financial ones, and how to manage the cognitive biases that can lead to poor financial choices.

"The Total Money Makeover" by Dave Ramsey - Ramsey offers straightforward advice on getting out of debt, saving money, and building wealth through seven "baby steps."

"The Little Book of Common Sense Investing" by John C. Bogle - The founder of The Vanguard Group offers simple advice on using index funds to build wealth, emphasizing the virtues of simplicity and low costs in investing.

Websites and Blogs

- Value Research Online (www.valueresearchonline.com) - Offers in-depth research, data, and analysis on stocks and mutual funds in India, helping investors make informed decisions.

- The Economic Times: Personal Finance Section (economictimes.indiatimes.com) - Provides news, analysis, and tips on personal finance, investments, and wealth management in India.
- Moneycontrol (www.moneycontrol.com) - A comprehensive resource offering financial news, data, and insights on the Indian market, including stocks, mutual funds, and personal finance.

Podcasts

- **"Paisa Vaisa"** - Hosted by Anupam Gupta, this podcast features discussions with experts on a range of topics related to personal finance, investing, and financial planning in India.
- **"The Rational Reminder Podcast"** - A weekly podcast on sensible investing and financial decision-making for Canadians and investors globally. While it focuses on Canada, the principles of long-term investing it discusses are universal.

Online Courses

- **"Personal Finance" by Coursera** - Offers a variety of online courses covering the basics of personal financial planning, investing, and managing personal finances.
- **"Financial Markets" by Yale University on Coursera** - Taught by Robert Shiller, this course provides an overview of risk management, behavioral finance, and the workings of financial markets, offering insights that are applicable worldwide.

By engaging with these recommended readings and resources, you can continue to build your financial knowledge and empower yourself to make more informed decisions. Remember, the journey to financial freedom is ongoing, and continual learning is key to navigating the complexities of personal finance.

About the Author

Rahul Goyal is the visionary author behind "Master Your Finances: A Comprehensive Guide to Financial Freedom in India." With an educational foundation that spans both business and law, Rahul embarked on his academic journey at GH Raisoni College, Nagpur, where he pursued a Bachelor of Business Administration (BBA) and a Bachelor of Laws (LLB). His passion for understanding the intricacies of leadership and organizational dynamics led him to further his studies at the prestigious London School of Economics, where he specialized in Leadership in Organisation.

With over a decade of experience in the Indian business landscape, Rahul has navigated the complexities of starting and running successful ventures in one of the world's most dynamic markets. His entrepreneurial journey is marked by a series of ventures that span various sectors, providing him with a rich tapestry of experiences and insights into the economic and legal nuances of doing business in India.

Rahul's expertise is not just rooted in his academic accolades or his entrepreneurial ventures; it is also deeply influenced by his personal journey towards financial literacy and independence. Having faced and overcome the challenges that come with managing finances in a volatile economy, Rahul has cultivated a profound understanding of what it means to achieve financial freedom in India.

"Master Your Finances" is more than just a book; it is Rahul's way of sharing his wealth of knowledge and experience with others who aspire to navigate the path of financial independence. Through this guide, Rahul aims to demystify the complexities of personal finance, investment, and economic resilience, offering readers a practical and insightful roadmap to financial empowerment.

Rahul is a firm believer in the power of education and empowerment. He is passionate about sharing his knowledge with others, whether through his writing, public speaking engagements, or as a mentor to budding entrepreneurs. His dedication to fostering financial literacy and independence is a testament to his commitment to making a meaningful impact in the lives of individuals navigating the financial landscape of India.

In his free time, Rahul enjoys reading, traveling, and exploring new technologies that have the potential to transform the business world. He is always on the lookout for innovative ideas and solutions that can drive growth, sustainability, and social impact.

Through his book, Rahul Goyal invites readers on a journey of discovery, learning, and empowerment. He believes that financial freedom is within reach for anyone willing to learn, adapt, and persevere, and he is dedicated to guiding his readers every step of the way.

Testimonials and Reviews for "Master Your Finances: A Comprehensive Guide to Financial Freedom in India"

"A Transformative Guide"
"Rahul Goyal's 'Master Your Finances' is a transformative guide that demystifies the complex world of personal finance in India. It's rare to find a book so rich in practical wisdom, yet so accessible. A must-read for anyone looking to take control of their financial future." - Arvind Upasani, Financial Educator and Author

"Empowering and Enlightening"

"This book is a beacon for those navigating the turbulent waters of personal finance. Goyal's expertise shines through in his actionable advice and compassionate guidance. 'Master Your Finances' is both empowering and enlightening, a true asset to anyone's financial literacy journey." - Shruti Muchhal, Entrepreneur and Investor

"Comprehensive and Insightful"

"Rahul Goyal offers a comprehensive and insightful exploration into achieving financial freedom in India. The book's structured approach, from basics to advanced financial planning, provides a clear path for readers of all levels. It's an invaluable resource that I will be recommending to my clients." - Priya Singh, Financial Planner

"A Roadmap to Financial Independence"

"In 'Master Your Finances,' Rahul Goyal has created more than just a book; it's a roadmap to financial independence. His practical advice, combined with real-life examples, makes the journey towards financial freedom achievable for the average Indian. An outstanding contribution to financial education." - Shailash Lamsonge, Business Analyst

"Engaging and Practical"

"I was thoroughly impressed by the engaging writing style and the practicality of the advice offered in 'Master Your Finances.' Rahul Goyal addresses the unique financial challenges faced by Indians with clarity and wisdom. This book is a testament to his extensive experience and deep understanding of personal finance." - Prashant Agrawal, Entrepreneur and Investor

"A Must-Have Financial Guide"

"As someone who has struggled with managing personal finances, I found 'Master Your Finances' to be an eye-opener. Rahul Goyal's approachable writing and practical strategies have given me the confidence to take charge of my financial destiny. This book is a must-have for anyone serious about financial freedom." - Amit Verma, Reader and Aspiring Entrepreneur

---

These testimonials and reviews reflect the impact "Master Your Finances: A Comprehensive Guide to Financial Freedom in India" has had on a diverse range of readers, from industry professionals to everyday individuals seeking to improve their financial literacy and independence.